The Power of Time Management: Strategies for Student Success

Johannes Meyer

Copyright © [2023]

Title: The Power of Time Management: Strategies for Student Success

Author's: Johannes Meyer.

All rights reserved. No part of this publication may be reproduced, stored in a retrieval system, or transmitted in any form or by any means, electronic, mechanical, photocopying, recording, or otherwise, without the prior written permission of the publisher or author, except in the case of brief quotations embodied in critical reviews and certain other non-commercial uses permitted by copyright law.

This book was printed and published by [Publisher's: Johannes Meyer] in [2023]

ISBN:

TABLE OF CONTENTS

Chapter 1: Understanding Time Management 06

The Importance of Time Management for Students

The Benefits of Effective Time Management

Common Time Management Challenges Faced by Students

Chapter 2: Setting Goals and Priorities 13

Identifying Personal Goals

Prioritizing Tasks and Activities

Creating Realistic and Achievable Goals

Chapter 3: Creating a Time Management Plan 19

Assessing Current Time Usage

Developing a Weekly Schedule

Allocating Time for Various Activities

Chapter 4: Effective Time Management Techniques — 25

Pomodoro Technique: Maximizing Productivity in Short Bursts

Time Blocking: Streamlining Your Schedule

Eisenhower Matrix: Prioritizing Tasks Based on Importance and Urgency

Chapter 5: Overcoming Procrastination — 31

Understanding the Psychology of Procrastination

Strategies to Beat Procrastination

Building Self-Discipline for Improved Time Management

Chapter 6: Managing Distractions — 38

Identifying Common Distractions

Techniques to Minimize Distractions

Creating a Productive Study Environment

Chapter 7: Effective Study Habits — 44

Time Management Techniques for Studying

Breaking Down Study Sessions

Utilizing Active Learning Strategies

Chapter 8: Balancing Academic and Personal Life — 51

Managing Coursework and Extra-Curricular Activities

Prioritizing Self-Care and Well-being

Seeking Support and Building a Supportive Network

Chapter 9: Time Management Tools and Apps — 58

Using Digital Calendars and Task Managers

Time Tracking Apps for Improved Awareness

Online Resources and Tools for Time Management

Chapter 10: Maintaining Long-Term Time Management Success — 64

Reviewing and Adjusting Your Time Management Plan

Developing Time Management as a Habit

Overcoming Setbacks and Staying Motivated

Conclusion: Embracing the Power of Time Management for Student Success — 70

Chapter 1: Understanding Time Management

The Importance of Time Management for Students

In today's fast-paced world, time management has become a crucial skill for students to master. With numerous responsibilities and an overwhelming amount of coursework to complete, students often find themselves struggling to keep up with deadlines and maintain a healthy work-life balance. This subchapter will delve into the significance of time management for students and provide strategies to help them enhance their timing sense.

One of the primary reasons why time management is essential for students is that it allows them to prioritize tasks effectively. By organizing their schedules and creating to-do lists, students can identify urgent assignments and allocate appropriate time to complete them. This not only ensures that important tasks are not overlooked but also helps students avoid the last-minute rush, reducing stress levels. Furthermore, effective time management enables students to make the most of their study sessions, as they are able to focus on one task at a time and give it their undivided attention.

Another crucial aspect of time management for students is the ability to balance academics, extracurricular activities, and personal life. Many students engage in various activities outside of their academic commitments, such as sports, clubs, or part-time jobs. By managing their time wisely, students can strike a balance between their academic responsibilities and their personal interests. This not only helps in personal growth but also teaches students valuable skills like discipline, prioritization, and multitasking, which are essential for success in the real world.

Moreover, effective time management allows students to develop a sense of self-discipline and accountability. By setting deadlines for themselves and adhering to them, students learn to take responsibility for their actions and outcomes. This skill is not only essential during their academic journey but also in their professional careers, where meeting deadlines and managing time efficiently are highly valued traits.

To enhance their timing sense, students can follow a few strategies. Firstly, they should create a realistic and achievable schedule, considering their individual strengths and weaknesses. Secondly, they should learn to say no to distractions, be it social media or unnecessary commitments, and allocate specific time slots for focused studying. Additionally, students should practice effective goal setting, breaking their tasks into smaller, manageable chunks. This not only boosts motivation but also helps them track their progress.

In conclusion, time management plays a vital role in a student's success. By mastering this skill, students can prioritize tasks effectively, maintain a healthy work-life balance, and develop discipline and accountability. By implementing the strategies outlined in this subchapter, students can enhance their timing sense and pave the way for academic excellence and personal growth.

The Benefits of Effective Time Management

Subchapter: The Benefits of Effective Time Management

Introduction:
In this subchapter, we will explore the incredible benefits that effective time management can bring to students. In today's fast-paced world, where time seems to slip through our fingers, developing a strong timing sense is essential for achieving success in academics and beyond. By implementing proven strategies for managing your time efficiently, you will unlock a world of opportunities and enhance your overall well-being.

Academic Success:
One of the primary advantages of effective time management is improved academic performance. When you have a clear schedule and prioritize tasks, you can allocate the necessary time for studying, completing assignments, and preparing for exams. By staying organized and focused, you will experience less stress and anxiety, ensuring that you make the most of your study sessions and retain information more effectively.

Reduced Stress and Improved Mental Health:
Effective time management minimizes the risk of feeling overwhelmed by deadlines and responsibilities, thereby reducing stress levels. When you have a balanced schedule and allocate time for relaxation and self-care, you allow yourself the opportunity to recharge and maintain a healthy mental state. This, in turn, enhances your overall well-being and enables you to approach your studies with a clear and focused mindset.

Increased Productivity:
With effective time management, you will experience a significant increase in productivity. By setting clear goals and deadlines, you can eliminate procrastination and make the most of your available time. When you develop a sense of urgency and discipline, you will find yourself completing tasks more efficiently, leaving room for additional activities or personal pursuits.

Improved Time Perception:
Developing a strong timing sense through effective time management allows you to accurately estimate the time required for various tasks. This skill is invaluable, not only in academia but also in your personal and professional life. It enables you to plan your days effectively, avoid last-minute rush, and make the most of every precious minute.

Enhanced Time for Personal Pursuits:
When you manage your time effectively, you can create space for activities that bring you joy and fulfillment. Whether it's pursuing hobbies, engaging in sports, or spending time with loved ones, effective time management allows you to strike a healthy balance between work and personal life. By dedicating time to things that matter to you, you will experience increased satisfaction and a greater sense of fulfillment.

Conclusion:
The benefits of effective time management are far-reaching, impacting every aspect of your life as a student. By implementing strategies to develop your timing sense, you will not only excel academically but also experience reduced stress, increased productivity, improved mental health, and the ability to pursue your passions. Embrace the

power of time management, and unlock the limitless possibilities that await you on your journey to student success.

Common Time Management Challenges Faced by Students

Time management is a critical skill that every student needs to master in order to achieve academic success. However, many students struggle with effectively managing their time, leading to stress, missed deadlines, and poor performance. In this subchapter, we will explore some of the most common time management challenges faced by students and provide strategies to overcome them.

One of the main challenges students face is a lack of awareness of their own timing sense. Some students have difficulty estimating how long tasks will take, resulting in poor planning and a tendency to procrastinate. To address this challenge, it is important to develop a realistic understanding of your own timing sense. Keep a record of how long it takes you to complete different tasks, and use this information to create a more accurate schedule. Additionally, break larger tasks into smaller, manageable chunks, and assign realistic timeframes for each.

Another common challenge is the overwhelming amount of tasks and responsibilities students have to juggle. Between classes, assignments, extracurricular activities, and social commitments, it can feel like there is never enough time in the day. To overcome this challenge, prioritize your tasks by importance and deadline. Use tools such as to-do lists or digital calendars to keep track of your commitments and set reminders in advance. By organizing your tasks and allocating sufficient time to each, you can ensure that nothing falls through the cracks.

Procrastination is yet another challenge that students frequently encounter. It is easy to put off studying or completing assignments until the last minute, leading to heightened stress levels and subpar work. To combat procrastination, try breaking tasks into smaller, more manageable parts and setting specific deadlines for each. Use time-blocking techniques to allocate dedicated study periods and hold yourself accountable. Also, eliminate distractions such as social media or unnecessary notifications during your study time.

Lastly, many students struggle with maintaining a healthy work-life balance. It can be tempting to spend all your time on academic pursuits, but neglecting self-care and leisure activities can lead to burnout. To achieve a balance, schedule regular breaks, exercise, and relaxation time. Make sure to allocate time for hobbies, socializing, and self-reflection. By taking care of your physical and mental well-being, you will be able to approach your academic tasks with renewed focus and energy.

In conclusion, time management challenges are common among students, but with the right strategies, they can be overcome. By developing an understanding of your timing sense, prioritizing tasks, managing procrastination, and maintaining a healthy work-life balance, you can enhance your productivity and achieve success in your academic endeavors.

Chapter 2: Setting Goals and Priorities

Identifying Personal Goals

In the fast-paced world we live in, it's easy to get caught up in the whirlwind of daily activities and lose sight of our personal goals. As students, it becomes even more crucial to manage our time effectively and align it with our personal aspirations. This subchapter aims to guide you through the process of identifying your personal goals and how they can be integrated into your time management strategy.

The first step in identifying personal goals is self-reflection. Take some time to ponder upon what truly matters to you in life. What are your passions, dreams, and ambitions? What do you want to achieve academically, professionally, or personally? By understanding your deepest desires, you can establish a clear vision for your future.

Once you have a general idea of your personal goals, it is important to set specific, measurable, achievable, relevant, and time-bound (SMART) objectives. Break down your goals into smaller, manageable tasks. For example, if your goal is to improve your grades, you can set specific targets for each subject or assignment. This will help you stay focused and motivated.

To enhance your timing sense, consider prioritizing your goals. Determine which goals are most important to you and allocate your time accordingly. It's essential to strike a balance between short-term and long-term objectives. While immediate tasks may demand your attention, don't neglect the bigger picture. Keep your long-term goals in mind and allocate time regularly to work towards them.

Additionally, develop a habit of regularly reviewing and reassessing your personal goals. As you grow and evolve, your aspirations may change. By periodically evaluating your goals, you can ensure that your time management strategy remains aligned with your current priorities.

Remember, identifying personal goals is a dynamic process. It requires self-awareness, clarity, and adaptability. Don't be afraid to dream big and aim high. Your goals should challenge and inspire you to reach your full potential. By incorporating your personal goals into your time management strategy, you will not only improve your efficiency but also find a greater sense of fulfillment and purpose in your academic and personal life.

In conclusion, identifying personal goals is a crucial step towards effective time management and student success. By taking the time to reflect on your aspirations, setting SMART objectives, prioritizing tasks, and regularly reviewing your goals, you can enhance your timing sense and work towards a future that truly aligns with your passions and ambitions. So, seize the opportunity and embark on this journey of self-discovery and goal-setting – the power to manage your time effectively lies within you.

Prioritizing Tasks and Activities

In the fast-paced and demanding world of academia, mastering the art of time management is crucial for student success. One key aspect of effective time management is the ability to prioritize tasks and activities. By understanding how to prioritize, students can optimize their productivity, reduce stress, and achieve their goals more efficiently.

Prioritization is all about making conscious choices regarding the importance and urgency of tasks and activities. It allows students to allocate their time and energy effectively, ensuring that they focus on what truly matters. Without proper prioritization, students may find themselves overwhelmed, constantly playing catch-up, and struggling to meet deadlines.

To begin prioritizing tasks and activities, it is essential to develop a clear understanding of your goals and objectives. What are you trying to achieve in the short term and the long term? By identifying your goals, you can align your tasks and activities accordingly, ensuring that they contribute to your overall success.

Once you have identified your goals, the next step is to evaluate the urgency and importance of each task. Urgent tasks are those that require immediate attention, typically with a specific deadline. Important tasks, on the other hand, are those that align with your goals and have a significant impact on your overall success. By evaluating tasks based on their urgency and importance, you can prioritize them accordingly.

One effective method for prioritizing tasks is the Eisenhower Matrix, which categorizes tasks into four quadrants: urgent and important, important but not urgent, urgent but not important, and not urgent or important. By using this matrix, students can identify tasks that require immediate attention, tasks that can be scheduled for later, tasks that can be delegated, and tasks that can be eliminated altogether.

Additionally, timing sense plays a crucial role in prioritizing tasks and activities. Some students naturally have a better sense of timing, allowing them to estimate the amount of time needed to complete tasks accurately. However, timing sense can be developed through practice and self-awareness. By keeping track of how long certain tasks take and making adjustments accordingly, students can improve their timing sense and allocate their time more effectively.

In conclusion, prioritizing tasks and activities is an essential skill for students seeking success in their academic journeys. By understanding their goals, evaluating the urgency and importance of tasks, and developing a sense of timing, students can optimize their productivity and reduce stress. With effective prioritization, students can navigate the demands of academia with confidence and achieve their goals efficiently.

Creating Realistic and Achievable Goals

Setting goals is an essential component of effective time management and is crucial for student success. However, it is equally important to create goals that are both realistic and achievable. This subchapter will provide students with valuable insights and strategies for setting goals that will help them develop a strong timing sense and ultimately achieve their desired outcomes.

One of the first steps in setting realistic and achievable goals is to identify what you truly want to accomplish. Take some time to reflect on your long-term aspirations, such as academic achievements or personal growth. This will give you a clear sense of direction and provide motivation to work towards your objectives. Once you have a clear vision, break it down into smaller, manageable goals that can be accomplished within a specific timeframe.

When setting these smaller goals, it is important to be realistic about what you can achieve given your current circumstances. Consider factors such as your academic workload, extracurricular commitments, and personal responsibilities. Setting goals that are aligned with your capabilities will prevent you from feeling overwhelmed and increase your chances of success.

Another crucial aspect of setting realistic and achievable goals is to ensure they are measurable. Assign specific criteria or milestones to each goal, so you can track your progress and stay motivated. For example, if your goal is to improve your grades, set a target grade for each subject or aim to complete a certain number of practice exercises each day.

Furthermore, it is important to prioritize your goals based on their importance and urgency. This will help you allocate your time and resources effectively, ensuring that you focus on the most critical tasks first. By doing so, you will be able to make progress towards your goals consistently and avoid wasting time on less important activities.

Lastly, remember to celebrate your achievements along the way. Recognize your progress and reward yourself for reaching important milestones. This will boost your motivation and confidence, providing the momentum needed to continue working towards your long-term objectives.

In conclusion, creating realistic and achievable goals is essential for developing a strong timing sense and ensuring student success. By identifying your aspirations, breaking them down into smaller goals, and considering your current circumstances, you can set yourself up for success. Remember to make your goals measurable, prioritize effectively, and celebrate your achievements. With these strategies in place, you will be well-equipped to manage your time effectively and achieve your desired outcomes.

Chapter 3: Creating a Time Management Plan

Assessing Current Time Usage

In today's fast-paced world, time management has become a crucial skill for students to achieve success. However, before diving into effective strategies, it is important to assess our current time usage and understand our timing sense. This subchapter aims to help students evaluate their current habits and identify areas for improvement in time management.

Assessing our time usage requires a self-reflective approach. It involves analyzing how we currently allocate our time throughout the day, identifying our priorities, and recognizing any patterns or habits that may hinder our productivity. By taking the time to assess our time management skills, we can gain valuable insights into our strengths and weaknesses, allowing us to make necessary adjustments.

To begin assessing your time usage, start by keeping a time log for at least a week. Record how you spend each hour of the day, noting specific activities and the duration of each. This log will provide a realistic snapshot of how you allocate your time and help you identify time-wasting activities or excessive time spent on non-essential tasks. Be honest with yourself during this process, as it will lay the foundation for improvement.

Once you have a clear understanding of how you currently spend your time, it's time to evaluate your priorities. Ask yourself questions like: Are you devoting enough time to your studies? Are you giving your health and well-being the attention they deserve? Are you engaging in activities that align with your long-term goals? Evaluating your priorities will help you prioritize tasks and eliminate unnecessary activities that are not contributing to your overall success.

Additionally, it is crucial to identify any patterns or habits that may be negatively impacting your time management. Are you easily distracted by social media or procrastination? Do you struggle to estimate how long certain tasks will take? Recognizing these patterns will enable you to develop strategies to overcome them.

Assessing your current time usage is an essential step towards improving your time management skills. It provides a clear picture of how you currently spend your time, helps identify priorities, and highlights any patterns or habits that may hinder your productivity. By understanding your timing sense, you can then implement effective strategies and techniques to optimize your time and achieve student success. Remember, time is a valuable resource, and by managing it wisely, you can unlock your full potential.

Developing a Weekly Schedule

One of the keys to achieving success as a student is effective time management. Without a well-structured schedule, it can be challenging to balance your academic responsibilities, social life, extracurricular activities, and personal time. In this subchapter, we will explore the importance of developing a weekly schedule and provide you with strategies to enhance your timing sense.

Creating a weekly schedule allows you to allocate specific blocks of time for various tasks and activities. By doing so, you can ensure that you make the most of your time and avoid feeling overwhelmed or rushed. Additionally, a schedule helps in setting realistic goals and deadlines, which are crucial for staying organized and meeting academic requirements.

To develop an effective weekly schedule, start by identifying your priorities. Consider your class schedule, assignment due dates, and any other fixed commitments. Allocate sufficient time for studying, completing assignments, attending classes, and participating in extracurricular activities. Remember to leave some time for relaxation and self-care to avoid burnout.

A helpful strategy is to break down larger tasks into smaller, manageable chunks. This approach allows you to make progress consistently and avoid procrastination. For example, if you have a research paper due in two weeks, allocate specific time slots each week for conducting research, writing drafts, and revising. By dividing the task into smaller parts, you can focus on each step individually, making it less daunting.

Furthermore, it is essential to be flexible and adapt your schedule as needed. Unexpected events or changes in workload are common, so having a flexible mindset will help you adjust your plans accordingly. Regularly reviewing and updating your schedule allows you to stay on track and ensure you are making the most efficient use of your time.

To enhance your timing sense, consider using tools and techniques such as time blocking, prioritization, and setting reminders. Time blocking involves allocating specific time intervals for different activities, ensuring that you stay focused and avoid distractions. Prioritization helps you identify the most important tasks and tackle them first. Setting reminders, whether on your phone or through apps, can serve as prompts to keep you on track and accountable.

In conclusion, developing a weekly schedule is vital for student success. By allocating time effectively, breaking tasks into smaller parts, and being flexible, you can manage your time more efficiently. Enhancing your timing sense through techniques like time blocking and prioritization will further boost your productivity. Remember, with a well-structured schedule, you can achieve a healthy balance between your academic commitments and personal life, ultimately leading to a fulfilling and successful student journey.

Allocating Time for Various Activities

In today's fast-paced world, managing time effectively has become a crucial skill for students. The ability to allocate time for various activities can significantly impact their overall success. Developing a strong timing sense is essential for students to excel in academics, extracurricular activities, and personal life. This subchapter aims to provide valuable strategies for students to optimize their time allocation and enhance their overall productivity.

Firstly, it is important for students to establish their priorities. By identifying their goals and objectives, they can align their activities accordingly. This requires setting realistic targets and breaking them down into smaller, manageable tasks. By doing so, students can effectively allocate time for each activity and ensure that important tasks are given the attention they deserve.

Secondly, students should create a schedule or a timetable. This helps in visualizing the available time slots and allocating them for specific activities. By having a well-structured schedule, students can avoid wasting time and ensure that all activities are accounted for. It is crucial to allocate time for studying, attending classes, completing assignments, and engaging in extracurricular activities. A well-balanced schedule ensures that students have sufficient time for both academic and personal growth.

Furthermore, students should learn to prioritize their tasks. By distinguishing between urgent and important activities, they can allocate their time accordingly. Urgent tasks require immediate attention, while important tasks contribute to long-term goals. By efficiently managing urgent tasks and dedicating enough time for important ones, students can avoid the last-minute rush and achieve better results.

Additionally, students must learn to avoid procrastination. Procrastination not only hampers productivity but also leads to unnecessary stress. By breaking tasks into smaller, manageable chunks and setting deadlines for each, students can overcome the tendency to postpone tasks. Allocating specific time slots for different activities helps in maintaining focus and discipline.

Lastly, students should allocate time for relaxation and self-care. It is crucial to strike a balance between work and personal life. By setting aside time for hobbies, exercise, and spending time with loved ones, students can recharge their batteries and maintain a healthy lifestyle. Allocating time for relaxation ensures that students remain motivated, focused, and productive throughout their academic journey.

In conclusion, allocating time for various activities is a key aspect of effective time management for students. By establishing priorities, creating a well-structured schedule, prioritizing tasks, avoiding procrastination, and dedicating time for relaxation, students can enhance their productivity and achieve success in their academic and personal endeavors. Developing a strong timing sense is not only beneficial during the student years but also sets the foundation for a successful and fulfilling life ahead.

Chapter 4: Effective Time Management Techniques

Pomodoro Technique: Maximizing Productivity in Short Bursts

In today's fast-paced world, time management is crucial for students striving to achieve academic success. With countless assignments, exams, and extracurricular activities, it can be overwhelming to manage one's time effectively. However, there is a powerful technique that can help students maximize their productivity in short bursts – the Pomodoro Technique.

The Pomodoro Technique, developed by Francesco Cirillo in the late 1980s, is a time management method that breaks work into intervals, typically 25 minutes long, separated by short breaks. This technique is based on the idea that the mind can maintain focus and concentration for a limited time, after which it needs a brief rest to recharge.

So, how does the Pomodoro Technique work? It's simple! Start by setting a timer for 25 minutes, also known as a "Pomodoro." During this time, commit to working on a specific task without any distractions or interruptions. Once the timer goes off, take a short break of 5 minutes. This break allows your mind to relax and prevents burnout. After completing four Pomodoros, take a longer break of 15-30 minutes to recharge and reflect on your progress.

The Pomodoro Technique is highly effective for students who struggle with maintaining focus and managing their time efficiently. By breaking tasks into smaller, manageable intervals, it helps to alleviate the feeling of being overwhelmed. Moreover, the regular breaks incorporated into this technique prevent mental fatigue and enhance overall productivity.

To make the most of the Pomodoro Technique, it is essential to create a conducive environment for studying. Find a quiet place where you can concentrate without distractions, such as turning off your phone or using website blockers to minimize temptations. Additionally, establish clear goals for each Pomodoro session to stay motivated and focused.

By implementing the Pomodoro Technique, students can improve their timing sense and accomplish more in less time. This technique not only enhances productivity but also promotes better time management skills, which are invaluable for academic success. So, why not give it a try? Take control of your time, break tasks into manageable intervals, and watch your productivity soar. Remember, success lies in the power of effective time management!

Time Blocking: Streamlining Your Schedule

One of the most crucial skills for student success is effective time management. As a student, you often find yourself juggling multiple tasks, assignments, and extracurricular activities. It can be overwhelming, and without a structured schedule, it's easy to get lost in the chaos. This subchapter will introduce you to the concept of time blocking and how it can help streamline your schedule, enhance your timing sense, and ultimately boost your productivity.

Time blocking is a powerful strategy that involves dividing your day into specific blocks of time dedicated to different activities. By assigning specific time slots for studying, attending classes, completing assignments, and engaging in personal activities, you create a structured and predictable routine. This technique helps you prioritize tasks, focus your attention, and achieve a better work-life balance.

To implement time blocking effectively, start by assessing your daily responsibilities and commitments. Identify your most important tasks and allocate specific time blocks for them. For example, if you have a challenging assignment due at the end of the week, block out a few hours each day to work on it. Be realistic and allocate sufficient time for each activity, considering your own capabilities and the complexity of the task.

Remember to include breaks in your schedule as well. Short breaks can help refresh your mind and prevent burnout. During these breaks, engage in activities that help you relax and recharge, such as going for a walk, practicing mindfulness, or chatting with friends.

When time blocking, it's essential to be disciplined and stick to your schedule as much as possible. Treat your time blocks as appointments with yourself and avoid distractions during these periods. Turn off notifications on your phone, close unnecessary tabs on your computer, and create a conducive environment for focused work.

While time blocking can help you streamline your schedule, it's important to remain flexible. Unexpected events or urgent tasks may arise, and you should be prepared to adjust your time blocks accordingly. Remember that the goal is to provide structure and optimize your productivity, not create a rigid timetable.

By implementing time blocking into your routine, you will develop a stronger timing sense, become more organized, and experience a sense of accomplishment. As a student, managing your time effectively is crucial for your academic success and overall well-being. Embrace time blocking and take control of your schedule to unlock your full potential.

Eisenhower Matrix: Prioritizing Tasks Based on Importance and Urgency

In today's fast-paced world, students are often faced with countless tasks and responsibilities, making it essential to manage their time effectively. One powerful tool that can help students prioritize their tasks and achieve success is the Eisenhower Matrix. This matrix, named after former U.S. President Dwight D. Eisenhower, provides a simple yet effective framework for categorizing tasks based on their importance and urgency.

The Eisenhower Matrix consists of four quadrants, each representing a different level of importance and urgency. The first quadrant is for tasks that are both important and urgent. These tasks should be tackled immediately since they require immediate attention and have significant consequences if not completed promptly. Examples of such tasks could include impending deadlines, urgent assignments, or important meetings.

The second quadrant is for tasks that are important but not necessarily urgent. These tasks are often related to long-term goals, personal growth, or important projects. While they may not require immediate attention, they should not be neglected either. Allocating time to work on these tasks regularly will help students stay ahead and achieve their long-term objectives.

The third quadrant is for tasks that are urgent but not necessarily important. These tasks are often distractions or interruptions that demand immediate attention but do not contribute significantly to student success. Examples could include responding to non-essential emails, attending to unimportant phone calls, or dealing with minor issues. It is crucial for students to minimize the time spent on these tasks to avoid getting sidetracked from their priorities.

Finally, the fourth quadrant is for tasks that are neither important nor urgent. These tasks are often time-wasters and should be eliminated or delegated whenever possible. Engaging in activities such as excessive social media scrolling, mindless internet browsing, or unnecessary meetings can eat up valuable time that could be better utilized for more important tasks.

By adopting the Eisenhower Matrix, students can enhance their timing sense and make better decisions about how they allocate their time and energy. Prioritizing tasks based on importance and urgency allows students to focus their efforts on what truly matters and eliminate unnecessary distractions. This not only improves productivity but also reduces stress and enhances overall student success.

In conclusion, the Eisenhower Matrix is a powerful tool that can help students manage their time effectively. By categorizing tasks based on their importance and urgency, students can prioritize their efforts, stay focused on their goals, and achieve greater success in their academic and personal lives. Embracing this strategy will not only enhance timing sense but also enable students to make the most of their limited time, leading to a more fulfilling and balanced life.

Chapter 5: Overcoming Procrastination

Understanding the Psychology of Procrastination

Procrastination is a common struggle that many students face when it comes to managing their time effectively. It is the act of delaying or postponing tasks, often resulting in increased stress levels and poorer academic performance. To overcome this challenge, it is essential to delve into the psychology behind procrastination.

One of the primary reasons why students procrastinate is the fear of failure. Many individuals believe that if they delay a task, they can avoid the possibility of not meeting expectations. This fear often stems from a lack of confidence or perfectionism, where students feel the need to produce flawless work. However, this mindset only exacerbates the problem, as the longer they delay, the more pressure they feel to deliver exceptional results in a limited timeframe.

Another psychological factor contributing to procrastination is the desire for instant gratification. Students are often drawn to engaging activities that provide immediate enjoyment, such as scrolling through social media or watching their favorite TV shows. In contrast, academic tasks may seem tedious and require more effort, making them less appealing in the moment. This disparity in pleasure leads to prioritizing short-term satisfaction over long-term success.

Additionally, poor time management skills can also contribute to procrastination. Students who struggle with managing their time effectively may find themselves overwhelmed with a pile of tasks, leading to a sense of paralysis. They may not know where to start or how to allocate their time efficiently, resulting in a cycle of procrastination.

To overcome the psychology of procrastination, students must first acknowledge and understand their underlying fears and motivations. Recognizing that fear of failure is a natural part of the learning process can help alleviate some of the pressure. It is crucial to adopt a growth mindset, embracing mistakes as opportunities for growth and improvement.

Developing strategies to combat instant gratification is also essential. Setting specific goals, breaking tasks into smaller, manageable steps, and rewarding oneself after completing each milestone can help create a sense of accomplishment. Moreover, eliminating or minimizing distractions, such as turning off notifications or using productivity apps, can enhance focus and productivity.

Lastly, improving time management skills is crucial for overcoming procrastination. Creating a schedule, prioritizing tasks, and utilizing time-blocking techniques can help students allocate their time effectively. Additionally, seeking support from classmates, teachers, or academic advisors can provide guidance and accountability.

By understanding the psychology behind procrastination and implementing effective strategies, students can overcome this common obstacle and improve their time management skills. Overcoming procrastination not only enhances academic performance but also reduces stress levels and cultivates a sense of achievement and self-discipline.

Strategies to Beat Procrastination

Introduction:
Procrastination is a common challenge faced by students, often leading to stress, missed deadlines, and a decline in academic performance. However, with effective strategies, you can overcome this habit and enhance your timing sense. In this subchapter, we will explore proven techniques to beat procrastination and manage your time more efficiently.

1. Develop a Schedule:
Creating a schedule is crucial for effective time management. Allocate specific time slots for different tasks, including studying, assignments, and leisure activities. By following a schedule, you will have a clear plan of action, which reduces the likelihood of procrastination.

2. Break Tasks into Smaller Steps:
Overwhelming tasks often lead to procrastination. Break down larger assignments into smaller, manageable tasks. This approach will help you feel more in control and motivated to start working on them. Celebrate small victories as you complete each step, which will further boost your timing sense.

3. Prioritize Tasks:
To avoid procrastination, prioritize your tasks based on their importance and urgency. Use techniques such as Eisenhower's Urgent/Important Matrix or the ABCD method to categorize your tasks. This way, you can focus on the most critical tasks first, ensuring you don't waste time on less important activities.

4. **Set Realistic Goals:**
Setting realistic goals is essential to maintain motivation and avoid procrastination. Break your long-term goals into short-term objectives and set deadlines for each. By setting achievable goals, you can measure your progress and stay on track with your studies.

5. **Eliminate Distractions:**
Identify and eliminate distractions that hinder your productivity. Turn off notifications on your phone, close unnecessary tabs on your computer, and create a dedicated study space free from distractions. By minimizing interruptions, you can maintain focus and complete tasks more efficiently.

6. **Use Time-Blocking Technique:**
Time-blocking involves allocating specific time blocks for different activities throughout the day. This technique allows you to dedicate uninterrupted time to specific tasks, enhancing your productivity. By adhering to this structured approach, you can effectively manage your time and overcome procrastination tendencies.

7. **Utilize Productivity Tools:**
Several productivity tools and apps can assist you in managing your time effectively. Tools like Pomodoro timers, task management apps, and note-taking tools can help you stay organized, track your progress, and enhance your timing sense.

Conclusion:
Procrastination can hinder your academic success and negatively impact your timing sense. However, by implementing these strategies, you can overcome procrastination tendencies and become a more

efficient student. Remember, effective time management is a skill that requires practice and perseverance. Embrace these strategies, and you will experience improved productivity, reduced stress levels, and greater success in your studies.

Building Self-Discipline for Improved Time Management

Introduction:
In today's fast-paced world, mastering the art of time management is crucial for success in any area of life. As students, it is particularly important to develop strong self-discipline to effectively manage your time and achieve academic excellence. This subchapter will guide you through the process of building self-discipline to enhance your timing sense and optimize your time management skills.

Understanding Self-Discipline:
Self-discipline is the ability to control your impulses, stay focused on your goals, and consistently follow through with your plans. It is the cornerstone of effective time management. Developing self-discipline requires practice, commitment, and a strong desire for personal growth.

Setting Clear Goals:
To develop self-discipline, start by setting clear goals for yourself. Clearly define what you want to achieve academically, and break down your goals into smaller, manageable tasks. Set deadlines for each task and create a schedule to stay organized. This will help you prioritize your time and ensure you are working towards your objectives.

Eliminating Distractions:
Distractions are the nemesis of self-discipline and can derail your time management efforts. Identify the distractions that often hinder your focus and develop strategies to minimize their impact. This could involve turning off notifications on your phone, finding a quiet study

space, or using website blockers to limit access to social media during dedicated study periods.

Creating Healthy Habits:
Developing self-discipline is closely linked to forming healthy habits. Establish a routine that promotes productivity and time management, such as waking up early, exercising regularly, and maintaining a balanced diet. These habits will provide you with the necessary energy and focus to stay on track and manage your time effectively.

Building Resilience:
Self-discipline can be challenging, and setbacks are bound to occur. Building resilience is key to overcoming obstacles and maintaining your timing sense. Learn from your failures, adapt your approach, and stay motivated to reach your goals. Surround yourself with supportive peers or mentors who can provide guidance and encouragement during difficult times.

Conclusion:
Building self-discipline is a lifelong journey that requires consistent effort and commitment. By setting clear goals, eliminating distractions, creating healthy habits, and building resilience, you can enhance your timing sense and become a master of time management. Remember, self-discipline is not about restriction but about empowering yourself to make the most of your time and achieve academic success. Start today, and let self-discipline be the driving force behind your time management journey.

Chapter 6: Managing Distractions

Identifying Common Distractions

In our fast-paced and constantly connected world, distractions seem to be lurking around every corner, making it challenging for students to stay focused and manage their time effectively. However, by learning to identify and address common distractions, you can regain control over your time and enhance your timing sense, ultimately leading to greater success in your academic endeavors.

One of the most prevalent distractions for students is technology. While smartphones, social media, and other digital devices offer numerous benefits, they can also be major time-wasters. To combat this, it is important to set boundaries and establish tech-free zones or specific time slots dedicated solely to focused work. By reducing the temptation to constantly check your phone or browse social media, you will be able to concentrate better and make the most of your study time.

Another frequent distraction for students is a cluttered physical environment. A messy desk or study area can make it difficult to concentrate and find the materials you need, leading to wasted time and increased stress. Take the time to declutter and organize your workspace, ensuring that everything has its designated place. A clean and tidy environment will not only enhance your focus but also reduce the mental strain associated with a chaotic setting.

Procrastination is yet another common distraction that hinders students' timing sense. Putting off tasks or assignments until the last minute not only adds unnecessary stress but also robs you of valuable time that could have been spent productively. To overcome this habit, break tasks into smaller, manageable chunks and set specific deadlines for each part. Additionally, consider using productivity techniques such as the Pomodoro Technique, which involves working in short bursts followed by brief breaks. By adopting these strategies, you can overcome procrastination and improve your overall timing sense.

Lastly, external distractions such as noise and interruptions can significantly impact your ability to concentrate and manage your time effectively. If you find yourself constantly interrupted by roommates, family members, or other external factors, try to establish boundaries and communicate your need for uninterrupted study time. Consider using noise-cancelling headphones or finding a quiet space where you can focus without disturbance. By creating a conducive environment, you will be better equipped to optimize your timing sense and make the most of your study sessions.

In conclusion, identifying and addressing common distractions is essential for students seeking to enhance their timing sense and improve their time management skills. By tackling technology distractions, decluttering your physical space, combating procrastination, and minimizing external interruptions, you will be able to reclaim control over your time and achieve greater success in your academic pursuits. Remember, mastering time management is not just about managing your tasks but also about managing the distractions that can derail your progress.

Techniques to Minimize Distractions

As a student, you know that managing your time effectively is crucial for your academic success. However, one major obstacle that often gets in the way of efficient time management is distractions. Whether it's the allure of social media, the constant ping of notifications, or the temptation to procrastinate, distractions can seriously hinder your ability to stay focused and productive. That's why it's essential to develop techniques to minimize distractions and make the most of your valuable study time.

One effective technique to minimize distractions is to create a dedicated study space. Find a quiet area where you can concentrate without interruptions. It could be a corner of your room, a local library, or a peaceful café. Make sure to keep this space clean, organized, and free from any distractions such as your phone or other electronic devices. By designating a specific area for studying, you train your mind to associate that space with focused work, making it easier to ignore distractions.

Another technique is to set specific goals and create a schedule. When you have a clear plan of what needs to be accomplished and when, you are less likely to succumb to distractions. Break down your tasks into smaller, manageable chunks and assign time slots to each of them. This way, you can track your progress and maintain a sense of urgency, reducing the temptation to veer off track.

Furthermore, it is crucial to prioritize your tasks. Identify the most important and urgent tasks and tackle them first. By focusing on high-priority tasks, you ensure that you are making the best use of your time and energy. This approach also helps in avoiding the feeling of being overwhelmed, which can lead to distractions.

In addition, consider implementing technology management strategies. While technology can be a valuable tool for learning, it can also be a major source of distractions. Turn off notifications on your phone or use apps that block certain websites or apps during designated study periods. By limiting your access to distractions, you create an environment that promotes focus and productivity.

Lastly, take regular breaks. Studies have shown that short breaks can actually enhance productivity and concentration. Use these breaks to recharge your mind and body, but be mindful not to get carried away. Set a timer to ensure you return to your work promptly.

By employing these techniques to minimize distractions, you can develop a stronger timing sense and improve your overall time management skills. Remember, successful time management is a key factor in achieving academic success, and by taking control of distractions, you set yourself up for greater productivity, improved focus, and ultimately, better grades.

Creating a Productive Study Environment

In order to succeed academically, it is essential for students to create a productive study environment. Having a designated space where studying takes place can greatly enhance focus, concentration, and overall efficiency in learning. In this subchapter, we will explore various strategies for creating an optimal study environment that will help students improve their timing sense and maximize their potential for success.

First and foremost, it is important to find a quiet and well-lit area for studying. Distractions such as noise, clutter, or poor lighting can significantly hinder productivity. A secluded room, library, or even a dedicated study corner at home can provide the necessary tranquility to concentrate fully on the task at hand.

Organization plays a crucial role in creating a productive study environment. Keep study materials, books, and supplies neatly organized and easily accessible. This will save valuable time that would otherwise be wasted searching for necessary resources. A well-organized study space fosters a sense of discipline and purpose, thus enhancing timing sense.

Ergonomics should not be overlooked when setting up a study environment. Ensure that your study area is comfortable and ergonomically designed to prevent physical discomfort or distractions. Invest in a supportive chair, a desk of appropriate height, and consider adding a cushion or backrest for added comfort during long study sessions.

Another important aspect to consider is the use of technology. While technology can be a valuable tool for studying, it can also be a major source of distraction. Minimize distractions by turning off notifications on your phone or computer, or consider using productivity apps that can help you stay focused and on track.

Furthermore, incorporating elements that inspire and motivate can greatly contribute to a productive study environment. Surround yourself with motivational quotes, posters, or images that remind you of your goals and aspirations. Personalize your study space to make it a place where you feel inspired and motivated to work hard and succeed.

Lastly, establish a study routine and stick to it. Consistency is key when it comes to developing good timing sense. Set specific study hours and create a timetable that allows for breaks and relaxation. By adhering to a routine, you will develop discipline and a sense of time management, which are crucial skills for student success.

Creating a productive study environment is essential for students aiming to improve their timing sense and achieve academic success. By following these strategies, students can optimize their study space, minimize distractions, and develop effective study habits that will ultimately lead to improved timing sense and increased productivity.

Chapter 7: Effective Study Habits

Time Management Techniques for Studying

Introduction:
Effective time management is a crucial skill for students looking to achieve academic success. By mastering the art of time management, students can ensure that they make the most of their study sessions, avoid procrastination, and maintain a healthy work-life balance. This subchapter explores various time management techniques specifically tailored to help students improve their timing sense and optimize their studying habits.

1. Prioritize and Plan:
Start by identifying your goals and prioritizing tasks based on importance and urgency. Create a study schedule or to-do list that outlines specific tasks and allocate realistic time slots for each. This will provide a clear roadmap for your study sessions and prevent you from feeling overwhelmed.

2. Break It Down:
Large tasks can be daunting, leading to procrastination. Break down complex assignments or projects into smaller, manageable tasks. This will make studying more approachable and allow you to tackle one piece at a time, enhancing your timing sense.

3. Use Time Blocking:
Time blocking involves scheduling specific blocks of time for different activities. Allocate dedicated study periods without distractions and stick to them. During these blocks, focus solely on studying, avoiding

social media, emails, or any other distractions. This technique helps you develop discipline and enhances your timing awareness.

4. Employ the Pomodoro Technique:
The Pomodoro Technique involves working in short bursts of intense focus, typically 25 minutes, followed by a short break of 5 minutes. After completing four Pomodoro cycles, take a longer break of 15-30 minutes. This technique helps prevent burnout, keeps you engaged, and improves your timing sense.

5. Eliminate Procrastination:
Procrastination is a common time management challenge for many students. Combat it by setting specific deadlines for each task, breaking them down into smaller steps, and rewarding yourself upon completion. Create a study environment free from distractions and use productivity apps or website blockers to stay focused.

6. Utilize Effective Study Techniques:
Optimize your study time by employing proven techniques such as active reading, summarizing key points, creating flashcards, or teaching the material to someone else. By using these techniques, you can enhance your understanding of the subject matter and make your studying sessions more efficient.

Conclusion:
Developing strong time management skills is essential for students to excel academically. By following these time management techniques, students can improve their timing sense, enhance their productivity, and achieve greater success in their studies. Remember, effective time

management is not about just working harder; it's about working smarter and making the most of the time available to you.

Breaking Down Study Sessions

One of the key factors in achieving success as a student is effective time management. This includes breaking down your study sessions into manageable chunks to maximize productivity. In this subchapter, we will discuss the importance of breaking down study sessions and provide strategies to help you improve your timing sense.

When it comes to studying, many students struggle with finding the motivation and focus to sit down for long periods. This is where breaking down study sessions becomes crucial. Instead of overwhelming yourself with hours of continuous studying, it is more effective to divide your study time into smaller, focused intervals. For example, you can aim for 30-45 minute study sessions followed by short breaks.

Breaking down study sessions into smaller chunks allows your brain to stay engaged and focused. It helps prevent burnout and enhances retention of information. Research indicates that shorter, frequent study sessions lead to better long-term memory. By spacing out your learning over time, you give your brain the opportunity to process and store information effectively.

To improve your timing sense and make the most of your study sessions, consider implementing the following strategies:

1. Plan Ahead: Create a study schedule and allocate specific time slots for each subject or topic. This will help you stay organized and ensure you cover all the necessary material.

2. Set Goals: Before each study session, set clear goals for what you want to accomplish. Having a specific objective will help you stay focused and motivated.

3. Use a Timer: Set a timer for each study session and adhere to it strictly. This will train your brain to work efficiently within allocated time frames.

4. Take Breaks: During your breaks, make sure to step away from your study area and engage in a different activity. This will refresh your mind and prevent mental fatigue.

5. Review and Reflect: After each study session, take a few minutes to review what you have learned and reflect on your progress. This will reinforce your understanding and identify areas that may require additional attention.

By breaking down your study sessions and adopting these strategies, you can develop a stronger timing sense and improve your overall productivity. Remember, effective time management is a skill that can greatly contribute to your success as a student. Start implementing these techniques today and witness the positive impact they have on your academic journey.

Utilizing Active Learning Strategies

In today's fast-paced world, time management has become a crucial skill for students seeking success in their academic pursuits. One aspect of effective time management that often goes overlooked is the implementation of active learning strategies. By actively engaging in the learning process, students can optimize their study time, enhance their understanding of concepts, and improve their overall academic performance.

Active learning strategies involve a hands-on approach to learning, encouraging students to participate actively in the learning process rather than passively absorbing information. This approach stimulates critical thinking, problem-solving skills, and deeper understanding of the subject matter. Here are some effective active learning strategies that can help students make the most of their study time:

1. Group discussions and collaborations: Engaging in group discussions allows students to exchange ideas, perspectives, and insights, promoting a deeper understanding of the material. By working together, students can clarify doubts, challenge each other's assumptions, and broaden their knowledge base.

2. Practical applications and real-life examples: Linking theoretical concepts to real-life scenarios helps students understand the practical relevance of what they are learning. By applying the knowledge to real-world situations, students can develop a better grasp of the subject matter and retain information more effectively.

3. Problem-solving exercises: Incorporating problem-solving exercises, such as case studies or simulations, challenges students to apply their

knowledge to solve complex problems. This not only improves their critical thinking skills but also enhances their ability to analyze and synthesize information.

4. Interactive technology: Utilizing interactive technology platforms, such as online quizzes, simulations, or educational games, can make the learning process more engaging and enjoyable. These tools provide immediate feedback, allowing students to self-assess their understanding and identify areas that require further attention.

5. Active note-taking: Instead of simply transcribing information, students should actively engage with the material while taking notes. This can involve summarizing key points, highlighting important concepts, or asking questions to clarify any uncertainties. Actively processing information during note-taking helps in comprehension and retention.

By incorporating these active learning strategies into their study routine, students can enhance their timing sense and make the most of their available time. Active learning not only improves understanding but also increases motivation and engagement, leading to better academic performance. So, challenge yourself to actively participate in your learning journey and unlock your full potential. Remember, time is a valuable resource, and utilizing active learning strategies is an investment that will pay off in the long run.

Chapter 8: Balancing Academic and Personal Life

Managing Coursework and Extra-Curricular Activities

In today's fast-paced academic environment, students often find themselves juggling multiple responsibilities. From attending classes and completing assignments to participating in extra-curricular activities, it can sometimes feel overwhelming to keep up with the demands of student life. However, with effective time management skills, students can successfully navigate their coursework and extra-curricular activities, achieving a harmonious balance while maximizing their potential for success.

One crucial aspect of managing coursework and extra-curricular activities is developing a keen timing sense. Timing sense refers to the ability to prioritize tasks, allocate sufficient time for each activity, and proactively plan ahead. By honing this skill, students can avoid procrastination, reduce stress levels, and accomplish more in less time.

To begin, it is essential to create a comprehensive schedule that includes both academic and extra-curricular commitments. Start by identifying fixed obligations such as classes, club meetings, or sports practice. Then, allocate dedicated time slots for studying, completing assignments, and reviewing material. Remember to factor in breaks and downtime, as overloading your schedule can lead to burnout.

Another helpful strategy is to break larger tasks into smaller, manageable segments. For example, if you have a research paper due in three weeks, set aside specific blocks of time for researching, outlining, writing, and editing. This approach prevents the overwhelming feeling of having a massive task ahead and encourages steady progress.

When managing coursework and extra-curricular activities, it is crucial to prioritize tasks based on their importance and deadlines. Use a prioritization system, such as the Eisenhower Matrix, to categorize tasks into urgent and important, important but not urgent, urgent but not important, and neither urgent nor important. This method ensures that you allocate your time wisely and focus on tasks that have the greatest impact on your academic and personal growth.

Furthermore, leveraging technology can greatly enhance your time management efforts. Utilize calendar apps, task management tools, and reminders to stay organized and on top of deadlines. Digital tools can help you set priorities, track progress, and provide timely notifications, allowing you to optimize your time for maximum efficiency.

Lastly, effective time management requires self-discipline and the ability to make conscious choices. Be mindful of potential time-wasting activities, such as excessive social media use or prolonged breaks. Instead, use your free time to engage in activities that recharge your energy, such as exercise, socializing with friends, or pursuing hobbies.

In conclusion, managing coursework and extra-curricular activities is a balancing act that requires a strong timing sense. By developing effective time management skills, students can navigate their responsibilities successfully, reduce stress, and achieve optimal results. Remember to create a comprehensive schedule, break tasks into manageable segments, prioritize wisely, leverage technology, and practice self-discipline. With these strategies in place, you can unlock the power of time management and excel in both your academic and personal pursuits.

Prioritizing Self-Care and Well-being

In today's fast-paced world, students often find themselves overwhelmed with various responsibilities and deadlines. As a student, it is crucial to understand the importance of prioritizing self-care and well-being to maintain a healthy balance in your life. This chapter will discuss strategies to help you develop a better sense of time management and improve your overall well-being.

Time management is not just about completing tasks and meeting deadlines; it is also about taking care of yourself. When you prioritize self-care, you are investing in your physical, mental, and emotional well-being. It allows you to recharge and be more productive in the long run.

To begin, it is essential to create a schedule that includes dedicated time for self-care activities. This could be as simple as setting aside a few minutes each day for relaxation or engaging in activities that bring you joy. Whether it's reading a book, going for a walk, or practicing mindfulness, find what works for you and make it a priority.

Another important aspect of self-care is maintaining a healthy lifestyle. Ensure that you are getting enough sleep, eating nutritious meals, and exercising regularly. These habits will not only improve your physical well-being but also enhance your cognitive abilities, making it easier to manage your time effectively.

Additionally, it is crucial to set boundaries and learn to say no when necessary. As a student, it is easy to get overwhelmed with social commitments and extracurricular activities. While it is essential to be involved, it is equally important to know your limits. Prioritize your well-being and learn to say no to activities that may be too demanding or not align with your goals.

Lastly, remember to take breaks and allow yourself time to relax and rejuvenate. Burnout is a common issue among students, and it can significantly impact your overall performance. Take short breaks between study sessions, engage in activities that help you unwind, and give yourself permission to rest.

By prioritizing self-care and well-being, you will not only improve your time management skills but also enhance your overall productivity and happiness. Remember, it is not selfish to take care of yourself; it is necessary for your success as a student. Take control of your time and make self-care a top priority in your life.

Seeking Support and Building a Supportive Network

In the fast-paced world of academia, it is crucial for students to not only manage their time effectively but also seek support and build a supportive network. Recognizing the importance of seeking support and building a strong network can greatly enhance a student's timing sense and overall success in their academic journey.

One of the first steps towards seeking support is acknowledging that it is okay to ask for help. Many students struggle with this concept, fearing that it may reflect inadequacy or weakness. However, seeking support is not a sign of weakness but rather a testament to one's commitment to personal and academic growth. Whether it is reaching out to professors, seeking tutoring services, or joining study groups, there are numerous avenues available for students to seek assistance and improve their timing sense.

Building a supportive network is equally important. Surrounding oneself with like-minded individuals who share similar academic goals can provide invaluable support and motivation. Joining student organizations, participating in extracurricular activities, and attending networking events are excellent ways to meet peers with similar interests and aspirations. These connections can serve as a source of inspiration, encouragement, and accountability, ensuring that students stay on track with their time management goals.

Moreover, building a supportive network extends beyond just fellow students. Engaging with professors, academic advisors, and mentors can provide guidance, advice, and additional resources to enhance one's timing sense. Professors, in particular, are valuable resources who can provide insights into effective time management strategies specific to their course requirements. By establishing a positive rapport with professors, students can also benefit from personalized feedback that can further improve their timing sense.

In addition to seeking support and building a supportive network, it is crucial for students to prioritize self-care. Taking care of one's physical and mental well-being is essential for optimal time management. Regular exercise, healthy eating habits, and sufficient sleep can significantly impact a student's ability to manage their time effectively.

In conclusion, seeking support and building a supportive network are vital components of developing a strong timing sense. Students should embrace the concept of asking for help and take advantage of the resources available to them. By surrounding themselves with a supportive network, students can find motivation, guidance, and accountability to enhance their time management skills. Additionally, prioritizing self-care ensures that students are in the best mental and physical state to manage their time effectively. Remember, success is not achieved in isolation, and seeking support is a powerful tool for student success.

Chapter 9: Time Management Tools and Apps

Using Digital Calendars and Task Managers

In today's fast-paced world, it can be challenging for students to keep track of their busy schedules and multiple deadlines. However, with the advent of technology, digital calendars and task managers have become invaluable tools for managing time effectively. In this subchapter, we will explore the benefits of using digital calendars and task managers for students with a keen sense of timing.

Digital calendars offer several advantages over traditional paper planners. Firstly, they provide a centralized platform where you can store all your important dates and deadlines. Whether it's upcoming exams, project due dates, or extracurricular activities, having all this information in one place allows you to have a comprehensive view of your schedule. Additionally, digital calendars often come with customizable features, enabling you to color-code events, set reminders, and share your schedule with classmates or study groups. This level of organization ensures that you never miss an important deadline or double-book yourself.

Task managers are equally crucial for students aiming to optimize their timing sense. These applications allow you to break down larger tasks into smaller, more manageable subtasks. By doing so, you can set specific deadlines for each subtask and monitor your progress. Task managers also offer features such as prioritization and categorization, helping you focus on the most critical assignments and allocate your time accordingly. Moreover, many task managers provide the option to create recurring tasks, ensuring that you stay on top of your daily, weekly, and monthly responsibilities.

Furthermore, digital calendars and task managers often sync across multiple devices, allowing you to access your schedule and tasks from anywhere at any time. This flexibility is particularly beneficial for students with hectic lifestyles, as it enables them to make better use of downtime, such as waiting for classes to start or commuting.

In conclusion, incorporating digital calendars and task managers into your time management arsenal can significantly enhance your timing sense as a student. The ability to centralize your schedule, set reminders, and break down tasks into manageable chunks will help you stay organized, meet deadlines, and reduce stress. Embrace technology and take advantage of these powerful tools to maximize your potential for success.

Time Tracking Apps for Improved Awareness

In today's fast-paced world, managing time effectively is crucial for students seeking success. With numerous tasks to juggle, assignments to complete, and deadlines to meet, it can be challenging to stay on top of everything. However, by utilizing the power of time tracking apps, students can greatly enhance their timing sense and achieve better results in their academic endeavors.

Time tracking apps are digital tools designed to help individuals monitor and manage their time efficiently. These apps offer a range of features that enable students to track their activities, set goals, and analyze their productivity levels. By utilizing such apps, students can gain a deeper understanding of their time management habits and make necessary adjustments to improve their efficiency and effectiveness.

One of the primary advantages of using time tracking apps is the ability to create a visual representation of how time is being spent. These apps provide detailed reports and analytics that allow students to see exactly how much time they are devoting to various tasks, such as studying, attending classes, or engaging in extracurricular activities. This awareness enables students to identify time-wasting activities and allocate their time more wisely.

Moreover, time tracking apps often include features like timers and reminders, helping students stay focused and on track. By setting timers for specific tasks, students can establish a sense of urgency and work more efficiently. Additionally, reminders can be set for important deadlines, ensuring that students never forget crucial assignments or exams.

Furthermore, time tracking apps often offer goal-setting functionalities. Students can set specific goals for each task or project and track their progress in real-time. This feature promotes a sense of accountability and motivates students to stay on track and complete tasks within the allocated time frame.

In conclusion, time tracking apps are powerful tools for students seeking improved timing sense and enhanced productivity. By utilizing these apps, students can gain a better understanding of their time management habits, identify areas for improvement, and make necessary adjustments to optimize their efficiency. With visual representations, timers, reminders, and goal-setting features, time tracking apps empower students to take control of their time and achieve academic success. Embrace the power of time tracking apps and unlock your true potential!

Online Resources and Tools for Time Management

In today's fast-paced digital world, effective time management has become a crucial skill for students seeking success in their academic endeavors. The good news is that there are numerous online resources and tools available to help enhance your timing sense and master the art of managing your time efficiently. These resources can assist you in prioritizing tasks, setting goals, and maintaining a healthy work-life balance. In this subchapter, we will explore some of the most valuable online resources and tools for time management that can revolutionize your approach to studying and boost your productivity.

1. Time-tracking apps: These apps help you monitor and analyze how you spend your time. By providing detailed reports and visual representations of your activities, they enable you to identify time-wasting habits and make necessary adjustments to improve your efficiency.

2. Task management platforms: These platforms allow you to create to-do lists, set deadlines, and track your progress on different assignments and projects. They help you stay organized, prioritize tasks, and ensure that nothing falls through the cracks.

3. Pomodoro timers: The Pomodoro Technique is a time management method that involves breaking your work into intervals, typically 25 minutes of focused work followed by short breaks. Pomodoro timers online can help you implement this technique and enhance your concentration and productivity.

4. Calendar apps: These apps enable you to schedule your activities, including classes, study sessions, meetings, and personal

commitments. By having a visual representation of your daily, weekly, and monthly schedule, you can better plan your time and avoid conflicts.

5. Online productivity tools: There are various online tools available that can help you streamline your work and collaborate effectively with peers. These tools include project management software, file-sharing platforms, and communication apps, which facilitate teamwork and task completion.

6. Online courses and webinars: Many websites offer free or paid courses on time management specifically tailored for students. These courses provide valuable insights, strategies, and techniques that can help you optimize your time and achieve academic success.

By utilizing these online resources and tools for time management, you can develop a strong timing sense, increase your productivity, and reduce stress. Remember, effective time management is not just about getting more tasks done, but also about finding a healthy balance between your academic pursuits and personal well-being. So, take advantage of these resources, experiment with different techniques, and find what works best for you in your journey towards student success.

Chapter 10: Maintaining Long-Term Time Management Success

Reviewing and Adjusting Your Time Management Plan

One of the key aspects of effective time management is regularly reviewing and adjusting your time management plan. As a student, it is crucial to develop a strong timing sense to ensure your success in academics. This subchapter will guide you through the process of reviewing and adjusting your time management plan, helping you optimize your study routine and achieve your goals.

Firstly, it is essential to understand the importance of reviewing your time management plan. By taking the time to reflect on your current strategies, you can identify what is working well and what needs improvement. This self-evaluation will allow you to make necessary adjustments, ensuring that you are using your time efficiently and effectively.

To begin the review process, start by analyzing how you currently allocate your time. Evaluate how much time you spend on different activities such as attending classes, studying, completing assignments, and engaging in extracurricular activities. This analysis will help you determine if you are dedicating enough time to each task or if there is room for improvement.

Next, consider the effectiveness of your study routine. Are you utilizing active learning techniques, such as summarizing material, quizzing yourself, or teaching others? Assess the impact of these strategies on your understanding and retention of the material. If certain techniques are not yielding the desired results, explore alternative methods and experiment with different approaches until you find what works best for you.

Additionally, review your time management tools and resources. Are you utilizing digital calendars, to-do lists, or productivity apps? Assess whether these tools are helping you stay organized and meet deadlines. If not, explore different options and experiment with various tools until you find the ones that align with your needs and preferences.

Lastly, after evaluating your current strategies and making necessary adjustments, it is vital to establish a routine for regularly reviewing and adjusting your time management plan. As you progress through your academic journey, your priorities, commitments, and study load will change. By consistently reviewing and adjusting your plan, you can adapt to these changes and ensure that your time is allocated effectively.

In conclusion, developing a timing sense is crucial for student success. Regularly reviewing and adjusting your time management plan allows you to optimize your study routine, identify areas for improvement, and adapt to changing circumstances. By dedicating time to this process, you will enhance your productivity, reduce stress, and achieve your academic goals.

Developing Time Management as a Habit

Time is a precious resource that must be managed effectively in order to achieve success in any aspect of life. For students, mastering the art of time management is crucial for academic excellence and personal growth. In this subchapter, we will explore strategies and techniques to develop time management as a habit, helping students enhance their timing sense and optimize their productivity.

1. Prioritize and Set Goals: The first step towards effective time management is to identify priorities and set clear goals. Students should determine their short-term and long-term objectives, breaking them down into smaller, manageable tasks. This will help them allocate sufficient time to each task based on its importance and urgency.

2. Create a Schedule: Developing a daily or weekly schedule is essential to stay organized and make the most of one's time. Students should create a timetable that includes dedicated study hours, extracurricular activities, and leisure time. By adhering to a schedule, they can establish a routine and ensure that each aspect of their life receives appropriate attention.

3. Eliminate Time Wasters: Time wasters, such as excessive use of social media, procrastination, or unnecessary multitasking, can significantly hinder productivity. Students should identify and eliminate these distractions to optimize their time. Utilize tools like website blockers or time-management apps to limit distractions and stay focused.

4. Set Deadlines: Setting deadlines for tasks helps create a sense of urgency and motivates students to complete their work on time. By establishing realistic deadlines, students can avoid last-minute stress and ensure that their work is completed with ample time for revisions and improvements.

5. Break Tasks into Smaller Chunks: Large assignments or projects can be overwhelming, leading to inefficient time management. Students should break down complex tasks into smaller, more manageable chunks. This approach allows for better planning and helps students allocate their time effectively, ensuring steady progress towards the final goal.

6. Learn to Say No: Students often find themselves overwhelmed with commitments and obligations. Learning to say no to non-essential tasks or activities is essential to maintain a healthy work-life balance. By managing their commitments, students can allocate sufficient time to their studies and personal growth.

Developing time management as a habit requires consistency and dedication. Students must understand that effective time management is not about working longer but rather working smarter. By applying these strategies and techniques, students can enhance their timing sense, increase productivity, and achieve success in their academic and personal lives.

Overcoming Setbacks and Staying Motivated

In the pursuit of success, setbacks are bound to occur. It is through these setbacks that we truly discover our strength and resilience. As students, it is crucial to develop the ability to overcome setbacks and stay motivated throughout our academic journey. This subchapter aims to provide valuable insights and strategies on how to effectively tackle setbacks and maintain a strong sense of motivation, particularly for individuals who struggle with timing sense.

One of the first steps in overcoming setbacks is to acknowledge that they are a natural part of life. Everyone faces obstacles and experiences moments of failure. Instead of dwelling on setbacks, it is important to adopt a growth mindset and view them as opportunities for learning and personal growth. By reframing setbacks in this way, students can approach them with a positive attitude and use them as stepping stones towards success.

Another important aspect is understanding the role of timing sense in our lives. For students who struggle with managing time, setbacks can often feel overwhelming. However, by implementing effective time management strategies, such as creating schedules, setting priorities, and breaking tasks into smaller, manageable chunks, students can regain control over their time and reduce the likelihood of setbacks.

Staying motivated throughout the ups and downs of academic life can be challenging, especially for those with timing sense difficulties. To combat this, it is crucial to set clear goals and establish a sense of purpose. By understanding why you are pursuing your education, you can find renewed motivation and push through setbacks. Additionally, surrounding yourself with a supportive network of peers, mentors, and family members can provide the encouragement and accountability needed to stay motivated.

Furthermore, celebrating small victories along the way is essential. By acknowledging and rewarding progress, students can maintain a positive mindset and fuel their motivation. Additionally, visualization techniques, such as creating vision boards or regularly envisioning success, can help students stay focused and driven.

In conclusion, setbacks are inevitable, but how we respond to them defines our journey towards success. By adopting a growth mindset, implementing effective time management strategies, setting clear goals, and staying motivated, students can overcome setbacks and achieve their academic aspirations. Remember, setbacks are not roadblocks, but rather detours on the path to greatness. Embrace them, learn from them, and grow stronger with every setback you face.

Conclusion: Embracing the Power of Time Management for Student Success

In today's fast-paced world, time management has become a crucial skill for achieving success in every aspect of life. As students, we often find ourselves juggling multiple responsibilities, from attending classes to studying, completing assignments, and participating in extracurricular activities. The ability to manage our time effectively can make all the difference in our academic journey and overall success.

Throughout this book, "The Power of Time Management: Strategies for Student Success," we have explored various techniques and strategies to help you develop a strong timing sense. We have discussed the importance of setting clear goals, prioritizing tasks, and creating a schedule that suits your individual needs. By adopting these time management principles, you can maximize your productivity, reduce stress, and achieve your academic goals.

One of the key takeaways from this book is the significance of setting realistic and achievable goals. By breaking down your long-term objectives into smaller, manageable tasks, you can create a roadmap that guides your daily actions. This approach not only helps you stay focused but also gives you a sense of progress and accomplishment as you tick off each task. Moreover, by prioritizing tasks based on importance and urgency, you can ensure that you allocate your time and energy effectively.

Another valuable lesson we have discussed is the importance of creating a schedule that aligns with your natural rhythms and preferences. Each person has their own peak times of productivity, and understanding these patterns can help you schedule tasks accordingly. Whether you are an early bird or a night owl, finding the optimal time for studying and completing assignments can significantly enhance your efficiency and retention.

By embracing the power of time management, you will not only excel academically but also gain control over your personal and social life. With effective time management, you can create a healthy work-life balance, allowing you to dedicate time to your hobbies, friends, and family without compromising your academic responsibilities.

Remember, time is a finite resource that cannot be replenished. By developing a strong timing sense and implementing the strategies outlined in this book, you can make the most of every minute and pave the way for your success as a student and beyond. Embrace the power of time management and witness the positive impact it has on your academic journey and overall well-being. Start today, and let time become your ally in achieving student success.